Fun and Easy
Drawing

Fun and Easy Drawing at Sea

Rosa M. Curto

Enslow Elementary
an imprint of
Enslow Publishers, Inc.
40 Industrial Road
Box 398
Berkeley Heights, NJ 07922
USA

http://www.enslow.com

INTRODUCTION

Making art is a fun way to express yourself. You can create your own world and the characters that live in it! There are many different tools you can use to make art, such as markers, colored pencils, crayons, and paint. It would be best to draw in pencil first so if you make a mistake, you can erase it and try it again. Then, once you are happy with your drawing, you can color it in any way you wish.

Here are some circles, triangles, ovals, and other simple shapes. You can find many of them at the bottom of the sea.

This book shows you how shapes can help you draw different things. Just follow the steps and use your imagination!

SOME TIPS BEFORE YOU START DRAWING:

- CHOOSE A QUIET AND WELL-LIT PLACE TO WORK.

- HAVE WHAT YOU NEED TO DRAW AT HAND.

- TAKE YOUR TIME.

- HAVE FUN!

SEA CREATURES

It is easy to draw a **STARFISH.**

Start with a dot. Draw five lines coming out from the dot.

Outline the starfish and color it in.

You can also draw a **SHELL.**

Now draw a **JELLYFISH** in three steps.

ANEMONES (uh-nem-uh-nees) come in many different shapes. Here is one example.

Here are two more shells to draw.

5

OCTOPUS

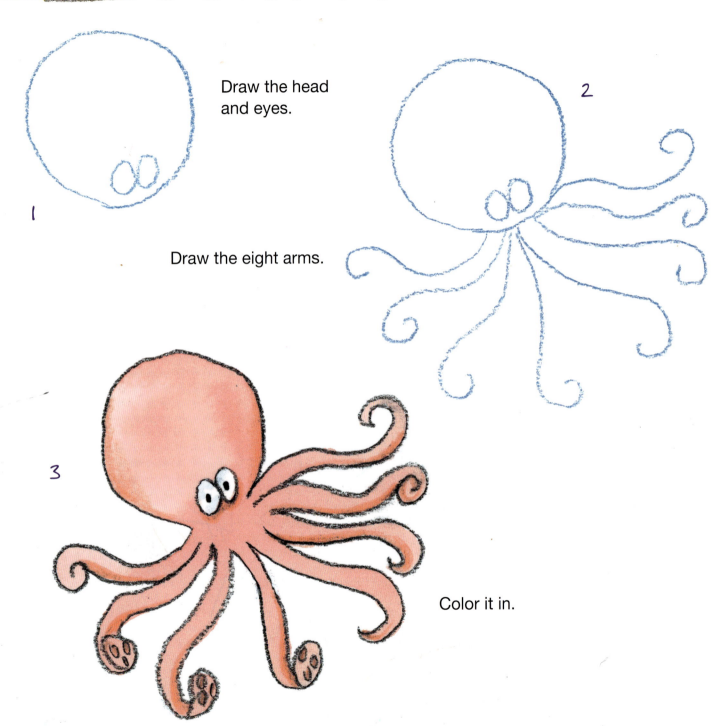

1

Draw the head
and eyes.

2

Draw the eight arms.

3

Color it in.

1

Draw another octopus.
These circles make up
the head, eyes, and body.

2

Draw the eight arms.

Finish the details
and color it in.

3

WHEN AN OCTOPUS FEELS IT
IS IN DANGER, IT SPRAYS A
JET OF INK. THE INK
MAKES THE WATER
DARK SO THE
OCTOPUS CAN
SWIM AWAY.

SEAL

1

Draw two ovals.

2

Draw four flippers.

Finish the flippers.

3

4

Color it in.

Draw two simple shapes.

1

2 Round off the shapes.

3 Add the flippers and nose.

BABY SEALS ARE SCARED OF WATER BECAUSE THEY CANNOT SWIM YET.

Color it in.

4

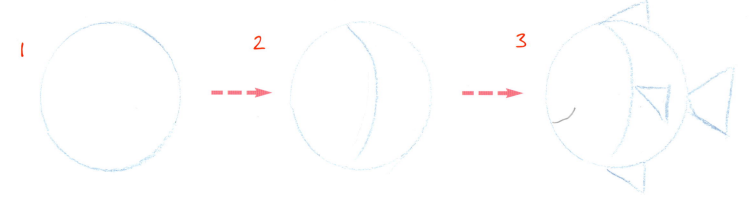

FISH

1 Draw a circle.

2 Draw a curved line inside the circle.

3 Draw four triangles for the fins and tail.

Draw an eye and a mouth.

Draw as many fish as you want and color them in.

4

A LARGE GROUP OF FISH THAT SWIM TOGETHER IS CALLED A SCHOOL OR SHOAL.

1 Draw an oval.

2 Add the fins and the tail.

3 Draw the eyes and mouth.
Color it in.

A SOLE IS A KIND OF FISH. IT IS FLAT
AND LIVES ON THE OCEAN FLOOR.
THE COLOR OF ITS BODY BLENDS
INTO THE SAND.

1 Draw an oval
and a triangle.

2 Draw two curved
lines inside the oval.

3 Finish the details
and color it in.

PENGUIN

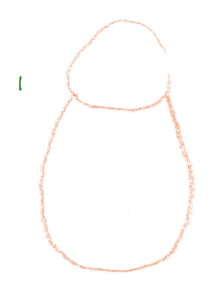

1

2

3

12

Here are two different penguins you can draw.

4

5

6

Just follow the six steps.
You will see how easy
it is to draw them.

1

2

3

4

5

6

PENGUINS CANNOT FLY.
THEY HAVE FLIPPERS
INSTEAD OF WINGS. THEY ARE
VERY GOOD SWIMMERS.

13

SQUID

Follow the seven steps to draw the squid.

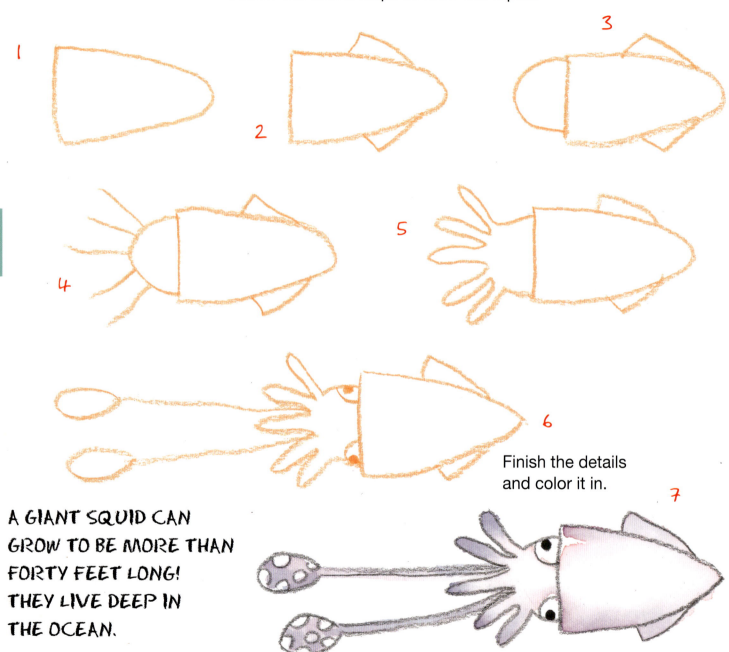

1

2

3

4

5

6

Finish the details and color it in.

7

A GIANT SQUID CAN GROW TO BE MORE THAN FORTY FEET LONG! THEY LIVE DEEP IN THE OCEAN.

SEAHORSE

1

2

3

Follow the five steps to make the seahorse.

4

Finish the details and color it in!

SEAHORSES COME IN DIFFERENT SIZES. THEY CAN BE HALF AN INCH TO EIGHT INCHES LONG.

5

WHALE

For the first whale, start with three simple shapes.

1

Round them off.

2

3

Draw the flippers and finish the tail.

4

Add details and color it in.

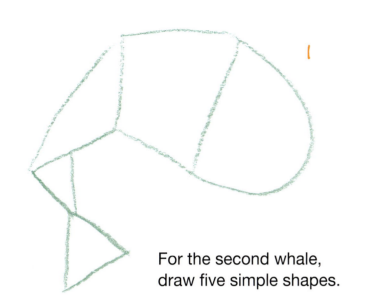

1

For the second whale,
draw five simple shapes.

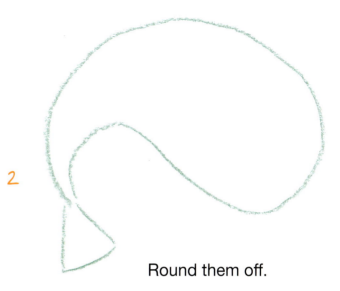

2

Round them off.

3

Draw the mouth
and flippers.

Finish the details
and color it in.

4

THE BLUE WHALE IS THE
LARGEST ANIMAL THAT HAS
EVER LIVED! IT CAN GROW TO
BE ONE HUNDRED FEET LONG!

DOLPHIN

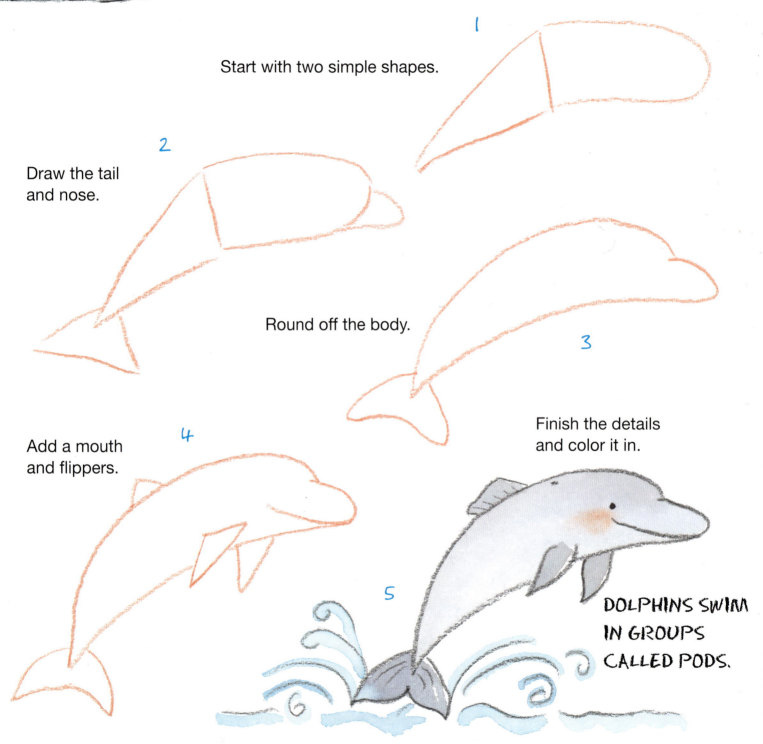

Start with two simple shapes.

1

2

Draw the tail and nose.

Round off the body.

3

Add a mouth and flippers.

4

Finish the details and color it in.

5

DOLPHINS SWIM IN GROUPS CALLED PODS.

18

SWORDFISH

1 Draw an oval.

2 Add the tail.

3

Draw the fins.

Draw an eye and the mouth.

4

A SWORDFISH'S BILL IS LONG AND FLAT. IT USES ITS BILL TO HELP IT MOVE THROUGH THE WATER.

Finish the details and color it in.

5

SHARK

Draw a shape similar
to a drop of water.

1

2

The tail looks like a half moon.

3

Add the fins and
the mouth.

Finish the details and color it in.

4

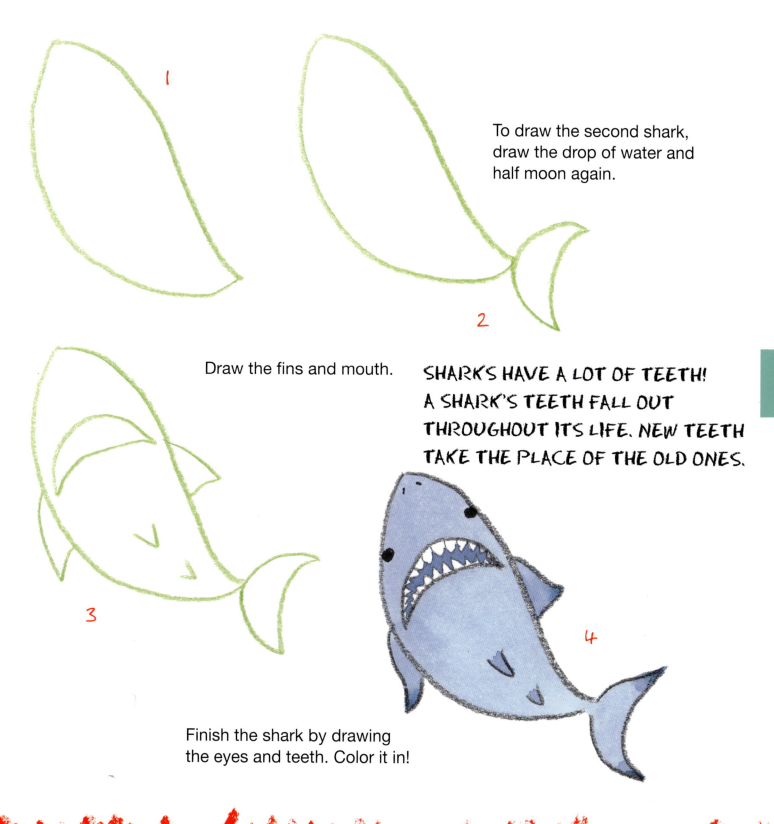

1

To draw the second shark, draw the drop of water and half moon again.

2

Draw the fins and mouth.

SHARKS HAVE A LOT OF TEETH! A SHARK'S TEETH FALL OUT THROUGHOUT ITS LIFE. NEW TEETH TAKE THE PLACE OF THE OLD ONES.

3

Finish the shark by drawing the eyes and teeth. Color it in!

4

SHIP'S CAPTAIN

Draw two circles, two small ovals, and two small triangles.

1

Draw a hat and pants.

2

Draw his neck and mustache.

3

4

Draw the jacket and the beard.

Finish the face and hands.

5

6

Color him in.

THE CAPTAIN IS THE LEADER OF THE SHIP.

23

SAILOR

Draw three simple shapes.

1

Draw the arms and pants.

2

Give him a hat and shoes.

3

Make the necktie.

Finish the arms and hands.

4

5

LONG AGO, SAILORS
COMMUNICATED
WITH EACH OTHER
USING FLAGS
AND CODES.

6

Finish the details and
color him in.

SWIMMER

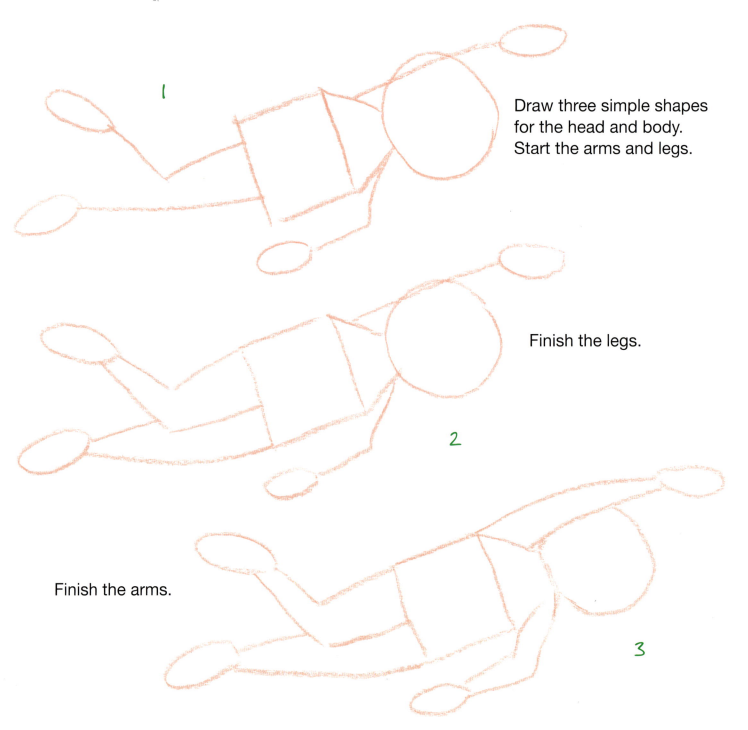

1

Draw three simple shapes
for the head and body.
Start the arms and legs.

Finish the legs.

2

Finish the arms.

3

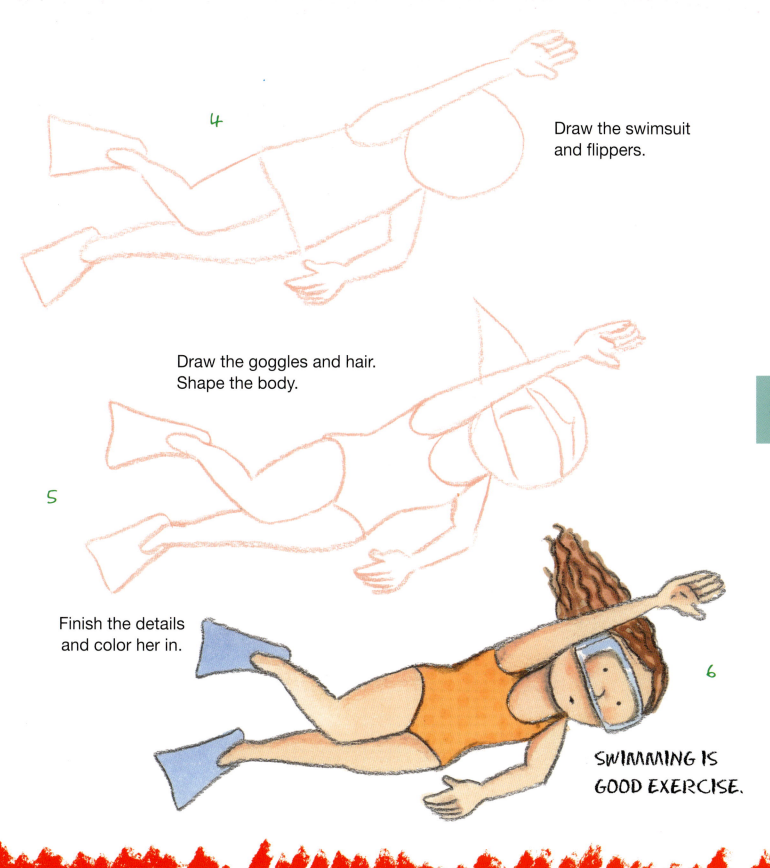

4

Draw the swimsuit and flippers.

Draw the goggles and hair. Shape the body.

5

Finish the details and color her in.

6

SWIMMING IS GOOD EXERCISE.

SUBMARINE

1

Draw an oval.

2

Draw the top.

3

Add windows all around.

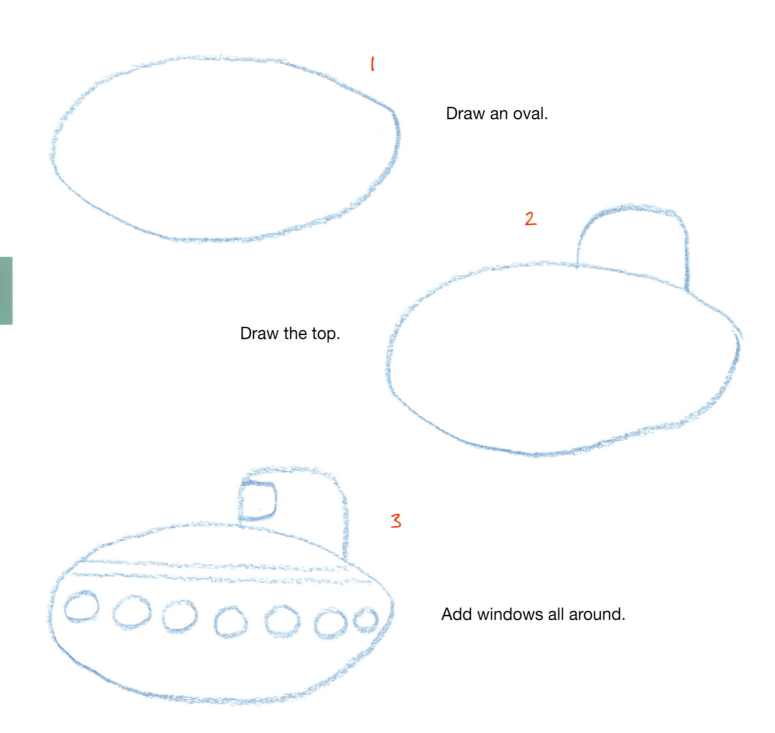

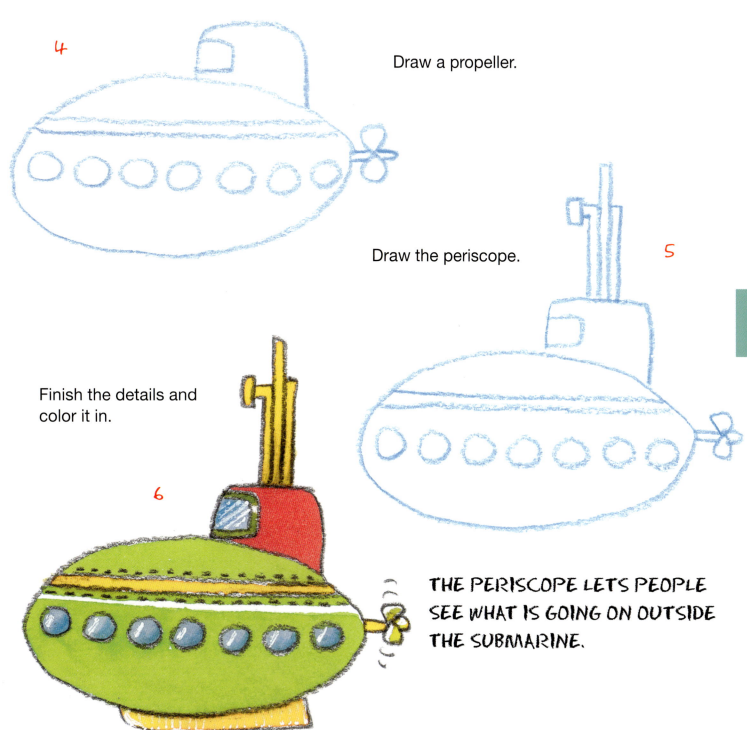

4

Draw a propeller.

Draw the periscope.

5

Finish the details and color it in.

6

THE PERISCOPE LETS PEOPLE SEE WHAT IS GOING ON OUTSIDE THE SUBMARINE.

 # SHIP

Draw a simple shape.

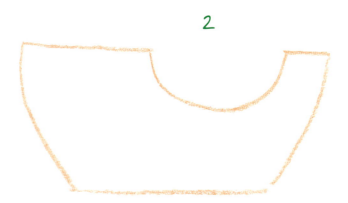

Draw a semicircle into the shape.

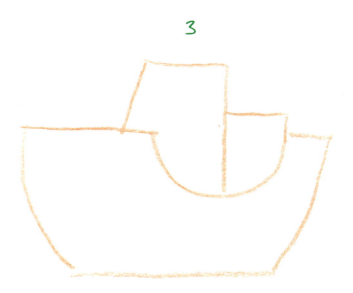

Add the cabin walls.

Draw the top of the cabin and smokestack.

The rectangular and round
windows are called portholes.

5

6

Draw two donuts to
make the lifesavers.

THE LEFT SIDE OF A SHIP IS
CALLED THE PORT SIDE.
THE RIGHT SIDE IS
CALLED THE
STARBOARD SIDE.
THIS DRAWING OF
A SHIP SHOWS
THE PORT SIDE.

Finish the details and color it in.

7

HOW TO DRAW THE SEA

A

To draw the sea, the first thing you must decide is whether it is calm or choppy.

Straight lines make the water calm (A).

Wavy lines make the water look like it is moving (B).

Points make the water look rough and stormy (C).

B

C

Look at drawing D. If you did not have the boat there, you would not have any idea how big the wave is.

DRAWING TO SCALE MEANS MAKING DIFFERENT OBJECTS DIFFERENT SIZES TO SHOW HOW BIG THEY ARE.

D

Light from the sky and surroundings gives the water its color.

A green sea usually has a lot of algae.

On a rainy, cloudy day, the sea looks dark and gray.

On a clear day, it looks blue.

At sunrise, the water looks yellow, red, and orange.

During a full moon, it is dark with some white and silver reflections.

At sunset, the sea can look pink and purple.

LOOK FOR PHOTOGRAPHS OF THE SEA. NOTICE THE DIFFERENT COLORS.

First make a list of the colors you see. Then draw the one you like the most.

HOW TO DRAW ICEBERGS

1

Look at the first drawing. The lines are very simple. Just color it in to get the second drawing. Almost all the color is in the sky. The walls of the icebergs are white.

ICEBERGS ARE HUGE BLOCKS OF ICE THAT FLOAT IN THE SEA. THEY CAN HAVE DIFFERENT SHAPES. THEY ARE MOST LIKELY TO BE FOUND IN THE ARCTIC OCEAN, NORTH ATLANTIC OCEAN, AND SOUTHERN OCEAN.

2

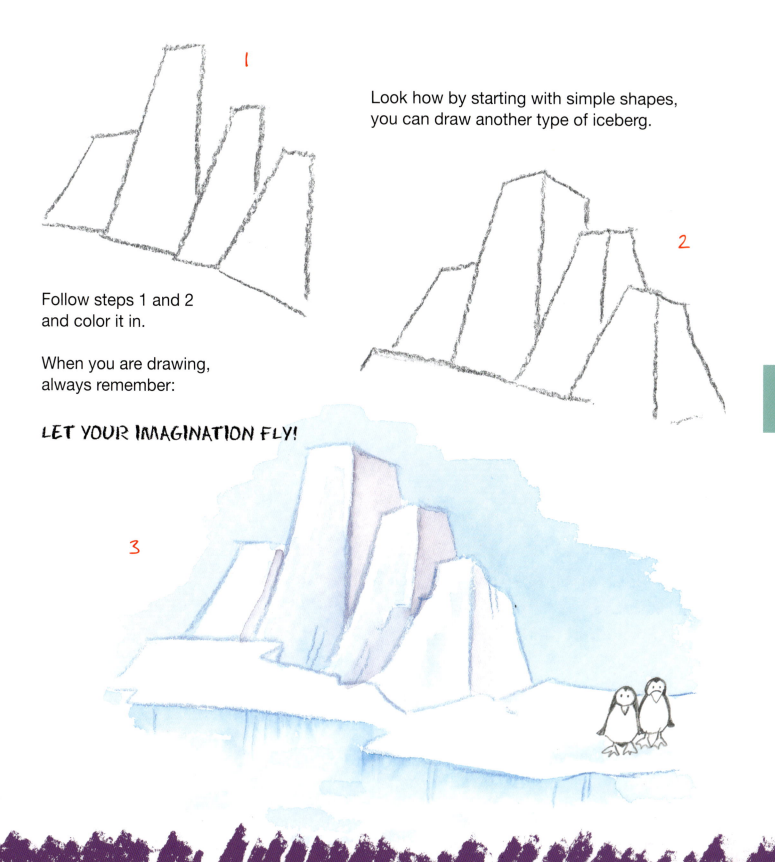

1

Look how by starting with simple shapes, you can draw another type of iceberg.

2

Follow steps 1 and 2
and color it in.

When you are drawing,
always remember:

LET YOUR IMAGINATION FLY!

3

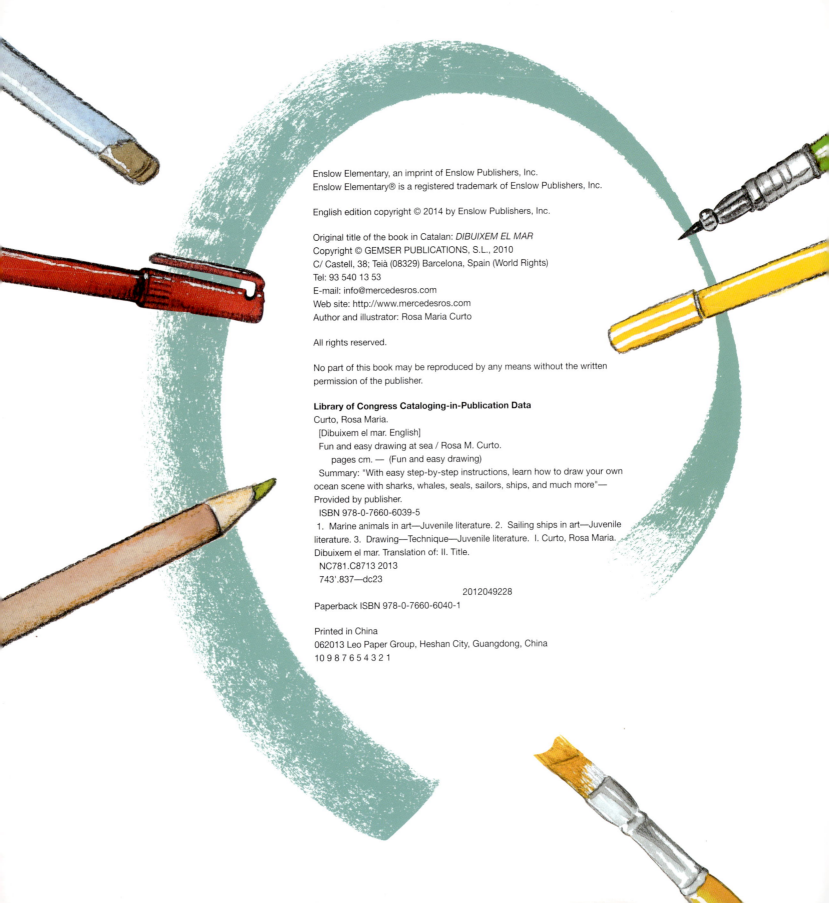

Enslow Elementary, an imprint of Enslow Publishers, Inc.
Enslow Elementary® is a registered trademark of Enslow Publishers, Inc.

Original title of the book in Catalan: *DIBUIXEM EL MAR*
Copyright © GEMSER PUBLICATIONS, S.L., 2010
C/ Castell, 38; Teià (08329) Barcelona, Spain (World Rights)
Tel: 93 540 13 53
E-mail: info@mercedesros.com
Web site: http://www.mercedesros.com
Author and illustrator: Rosa Maria Curto

Library of Congress Cataloging-in-Publication Data
Curto, Rosa Maria.
 [Dibuixem el mar. English]
 Fun and easy drawing at sea / Rosa M. Curto.
     pages cm. — (Fun and easy drawing)
 Summary: "With easy step-by-step instructions, learn how to draw your own
ocean scene with sharks, whales, seals, sailors, ships, and much more"—
Provided by publisher.
 ISBN 978-0-7660-6039-5
 1. Marine animals in art—Juvenile literature. 2. Sailing ships in art—Juvenile
literature. 3. Drawing—Technique—Juvenile literature. I. Curto, Rosa Maria.
Dibuixem el mar. Translation of: II. Title.
 NC781.C8713 2013
 743'.837—dc23
                                                    2012049228
Paperback ISBN 978-0-7660-6040-1

Printed in China
062013 Leo Paper Group, Heshan City, Guangdong, China
10 9 8 7 6 5 4 3 2 1